T0132002

Skin, Skin, Wonderful Skin

Archway Publishing books may be ordered through booksellers or by contacting:

Archway Publishing
1663 Liberty Drive
Bloomington, IN 47403
www.archwaypublishing.com
1 (888) 242-5904

ISBN: 978-1-4808-6712-3 (sc)
ISBN: 978-1-4808-6711-6 (e)

Print information available on the last page.

Archway Publishing rev. date: 10/30/2018

Skin, Skin, Wonderful Skin

Danby Whitmore

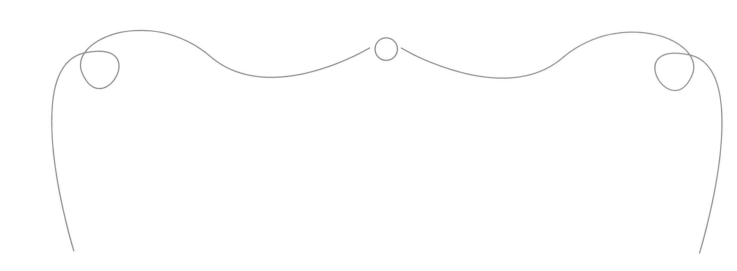

Skin, skin, wonderful skin

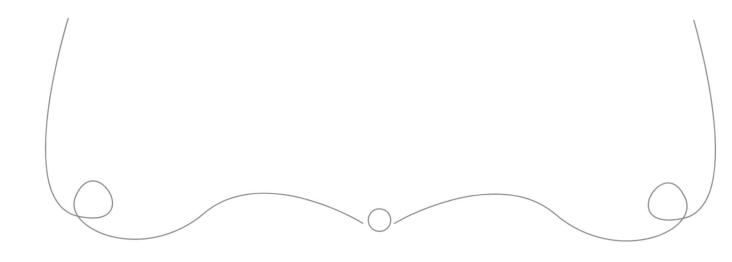

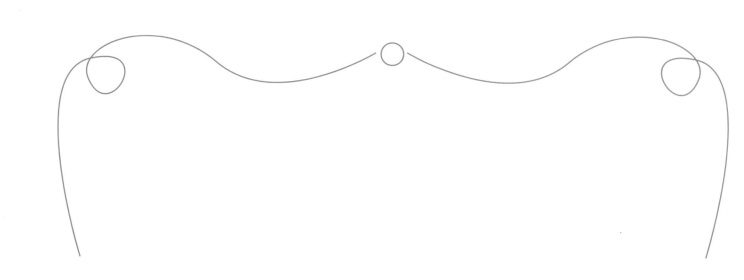

It comes in many shades,
colors, hues

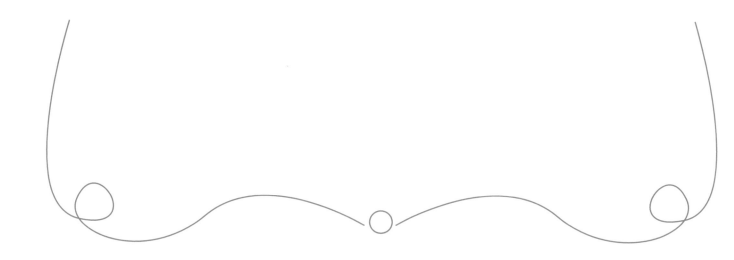

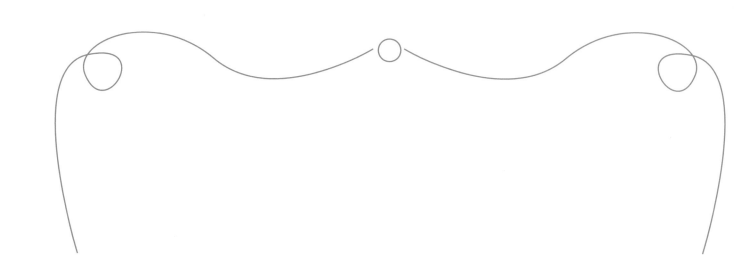

To make a rainbow of joy

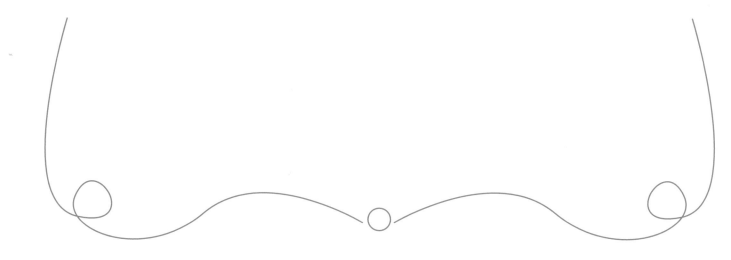

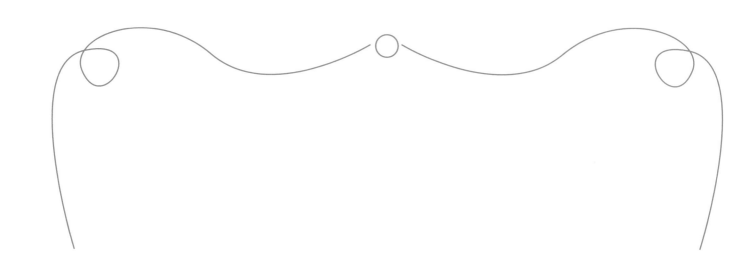

There is golden brown

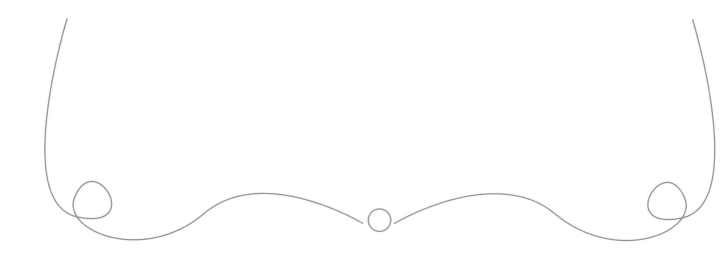

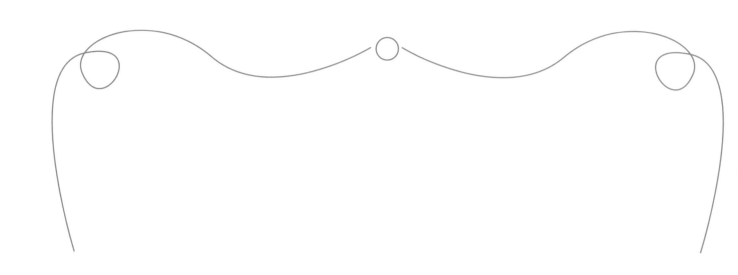

Yellow, white

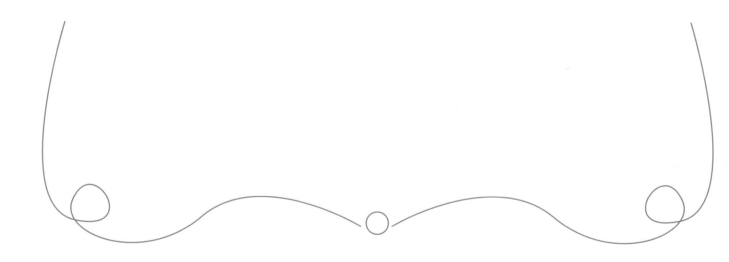

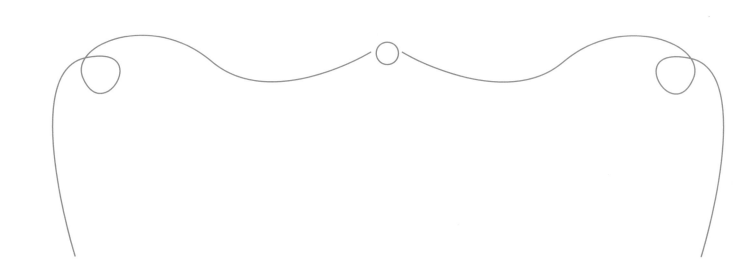

Black as night

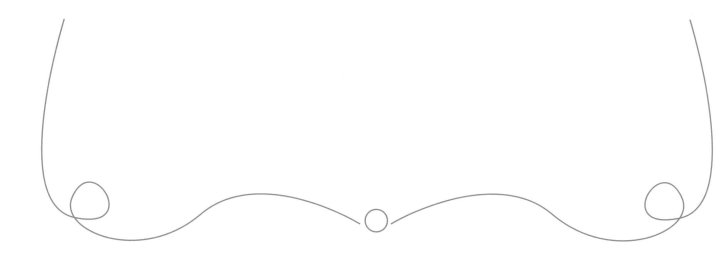

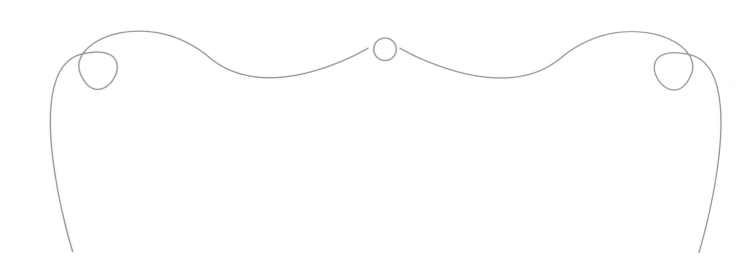

And orange, red, tan

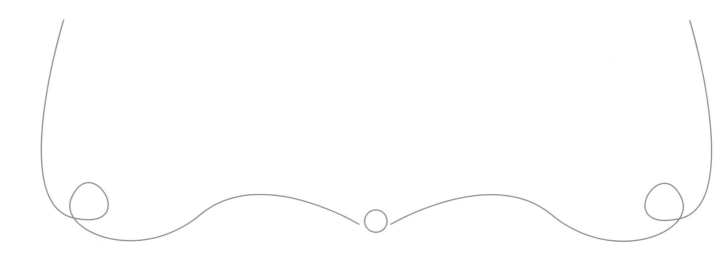

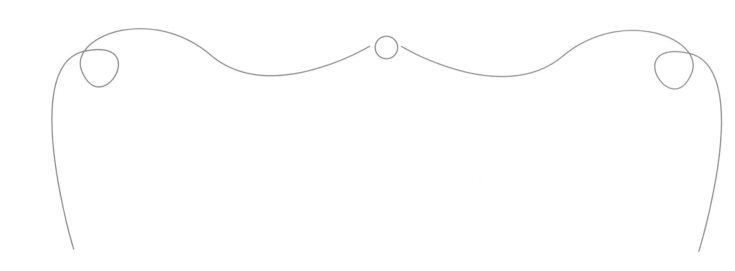

It is beautiful to see

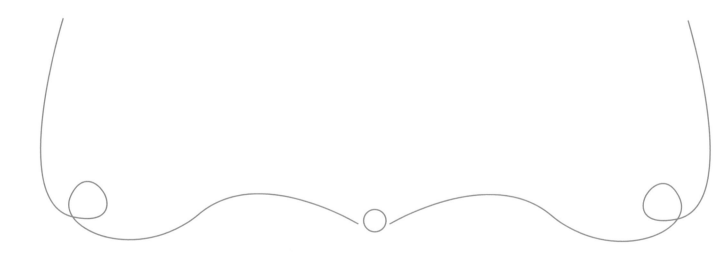

So many colors

All beautiful

You and me.

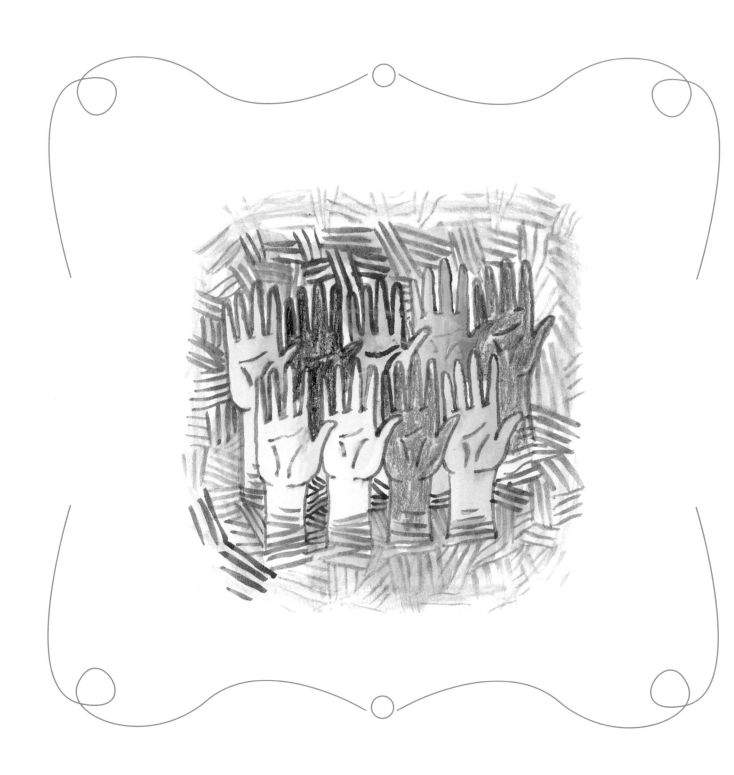

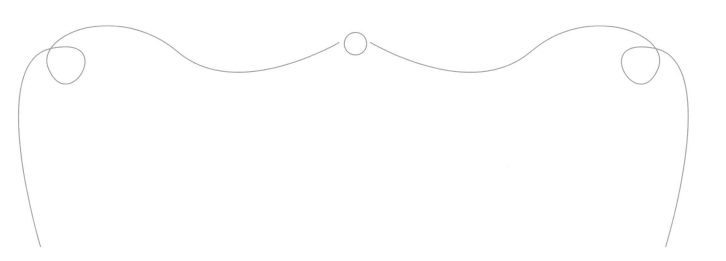

Adam Truitt, Illustrator

Is a resident of Ipswich Massachusetts. He attended Ipswich High School where he garnered many art awards and went onto MassART from which he graduated with a BFA in Fine Arts in 2015. His inspiration derives from a mother who is a captivating storyteller and father who is an excellent craftsman woodworker. Adam works in illustration, sculpture and film.

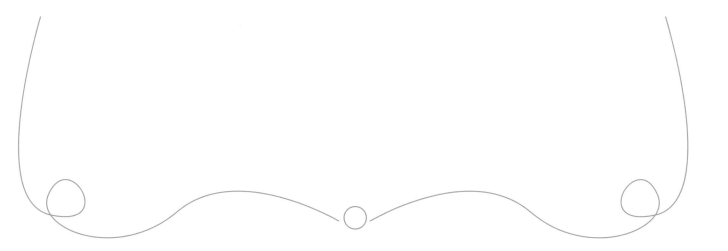

Printed in the United States
By Bookmasters